# HANON-SCHAUM

MW01012267

### The Purpose of the Hanon-Schaum Edition

Charles-Louis Hanon (1820–1900) was a French pianist, composer, and pedagogue who wrote important piano studies. His *60 Progressive Studies* became a standard piano method all over the world. His collections of exercises and studies range from easy and progressive to virtuoso. The Hanon-Schaum Edition is based on selections from *Le Pianiste-Virtuose*, one of the best known and most widely used sets of exercises ever composed. These études are comprised of patterns that move up and down the keyboard, each specifically composed to help students acquire speed and strength. Special emphasis is placed on equal development of both hands. The technical points are equally divided between the right and left hands. The exercises are purposely brief, thereby avoiding stiffness and tension. Using the Hanon-Schaum exercises will improve piano technic when used in conjunction with a program of balanced piano repertoire.

Editor: Gail Lew
Production Coordinator: Karl Bork
Cover Illustration: Magdi Rodríguez
Cover Design: María A. Chenique

# Preface

The study of the piano is so universal at the present time, and good pianists are so numerous, that mediocrity on this instrument is no longer tolerated. The result is that it is necessary to study the piano eight or ten years before attempting to play a piece of moderate difficulty, even before amateurs.

How few people are able to devote so many years to the study of this instrument! It often happens that for want of sufficient practice, the execution is uneven and faulty. The left hand is impeded by many of the more difficult passages, and fourth and fifth fingers are almost useless for want of special exercises. These fingers are always weaker than the others, and if the pupil comes across any passages with octaves, shakes, or trills, he or she executes them with difficulty and fatigue. The result is that the rendering is incorrect and lacking in expression.

For some years, we have been seeking to obviate this state of things by trying to collect in one work special exercises that will enable pupils to complete their pianistic studies in a much shorter time.

To attain this object, it was necessary to solve the following problem: If the five fingers of each hand were equally developed, they would be able to execute anything that has been written for the piano, and the only remaining difficulty would be that of the fingering, which could be overcome readily. The solution of this problem is to be found in *Le Pianiste Virtuose* in 60 exercises.

In this volume are the exercises necessary for the acquirement of flexibility, strength, perfect independence, and equality of the fingers, as well as suppleness of the wrists, all of these qualities being indispensable to the acquisition of a fine execution. Moreover, these exercises are calculated to make the left hand as capable as the right. These studies are interesting and do not tire the student as do most five-finger exercises, which are so monotonous that the perseverance and courage of a great artist are required to practice them.

These exercises are written in such a manner that, after having seen them a few times, the student can play them rapidly enough to render them excellent practice for the fingers without the loss of time in studying them.

If desired, all of these exercises may be played by several performers on a number of pianos simultaneously, creating a spirit of emulation among the students and accustoming them to ensemble playing.

In this book are all sorts of difficulties arranged so that in each successive exercise, the fingers find rest from the fatigue of the preceding one. The result of this combination is that, without extra effort or fatigue, all mechanical difficulties can be surmounted, and after such practice a surprising improvement is shown.

This work is intended for all students of the piano. After the student has spent one year in study, he or she may take it up with success. More advanced students will master these exercises in a very short time and, upon completion, will no longer suffer from stiffness in the fingers or the wrists. This will enable them to overcome the greatest mechanical difficulties.

In order to keep up their execution, pianists or teachers who have not had sufficient time to practice need only to play these exercises for some hours in order to regain the flexibility of their fingers. The whole of this volume can be played through in one hour, and as soon as it is mastered well and practiced daily for some time, difficulties will disappear as if by enchantment and the result will be the crisp, light, delicate touch that is the secret of great artists.

To sum up, we present this work as supplying a key to all difficulties of execution. We therefore believe that we are rendering a real service to young pianists, to teachers, and to directors of schools in proposing that they adopt our work, *Le Pianiste Virtuose.*

*Charles-Louis Hanon*

# Practice Suggestions

In re-editing the Hanon studies for teaching purposes, Mr. Schaum has provided the following advantages:

1. The exercises may be introduced at an earlier stage in the student's study of piano.

2. The studies are written in eighth notes instead of sixteenth notes, allowing for greater ease of reading.

3. Right hand and left hand are played two octaves apart instead of one octave. This improves posture and playing position.

4. Each exercise is condensed to sixteen measures each instead of thirty-two measures each. The shorter length of the exercises makes it easier for the students to review previous exercises each day along with the current exercise they are studying.

5. The sophisticated look of this edition makes it equally suitable for the adult student as well as the younger student.

When practicing the Hanon-Schaum exercises, the student should play them *forte (f)*. Once the exercises have been practiced *forte*, then reduce the volume to *piano (p)* and *pianissimo (pp)*. Practicing *forte (f)* will help the student acquire finger independence and strength. Good finger technique requires individual finger strength.

The *legato* touch should be stressed first. Other touches (for instance, *staccato* and *portato*) may be applied as the studies are reviewed.

For additional variety, the exercises may be played as follows:

1. Repeat the ascending section an *octave* higher, and repeat the descending section an *octave* lower.

2. Transpose the exercises to other keys.

3. Play the exercises using different rhythmic patterns (i.e., ♪.♪).

4. Play the left hand *staccato* and the right hand *legato*.

5. Play the left hand *legato* and the right hand *staccato*.

# No. 1

> *Directions: Play one exercise a week practicing it five times daily. While each new exercise is being mastered, keep reviewing the old ones once each day. Do this until the entire book has been learned.*

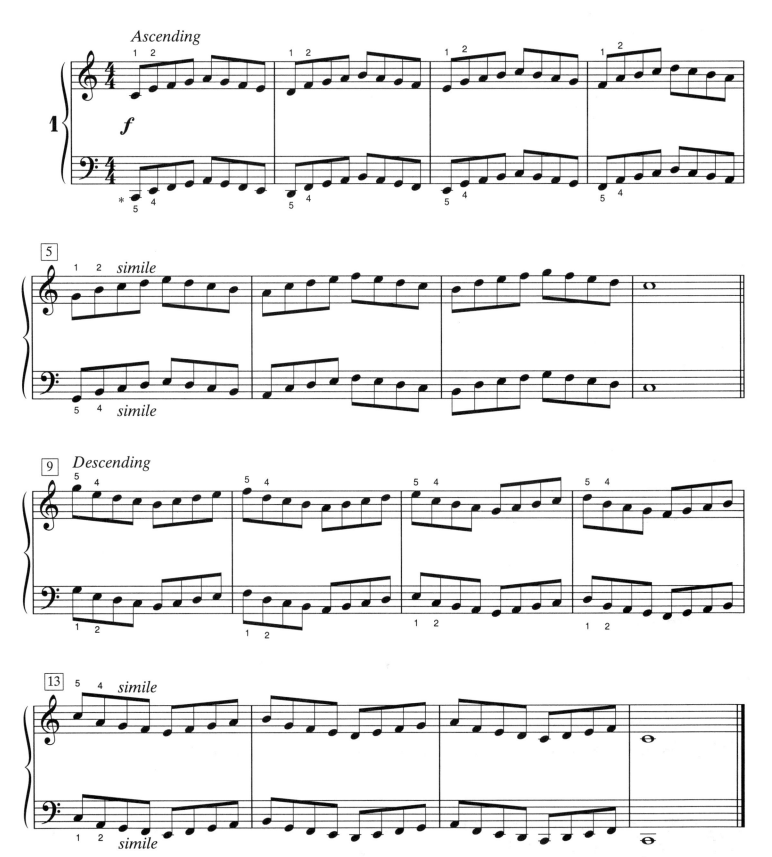

*Note: The left hand plays the same notes as the right hand, only two octaves lower. This is true for the entire book.

# No. 2

*Directions: Play exercise No. 2 five times a day and review exercise No. 1 once a day.*

EL00208A

# No. 3

Directions: *Play exercise No. 3 five times daily and review exercises No. 1 and No. 2 once daily.*

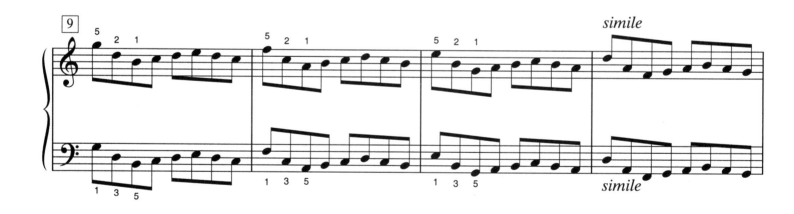

EL00208A

# No. 4

*Directions: Always practice the new exercise five times daily and review each old exercise once a day.*
*Follow this plan for the entire book.*

# No. 5

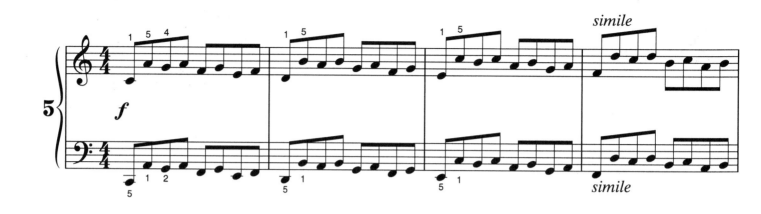

# No. 6

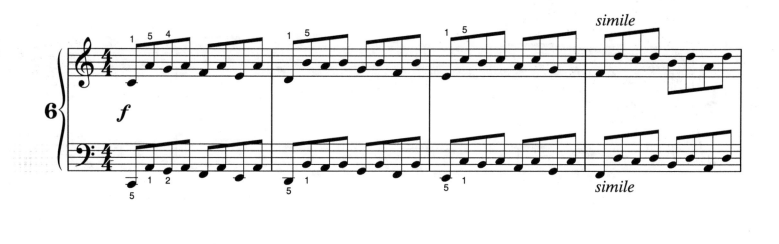

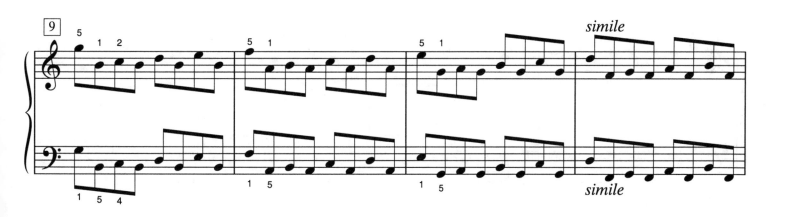

# No. 7

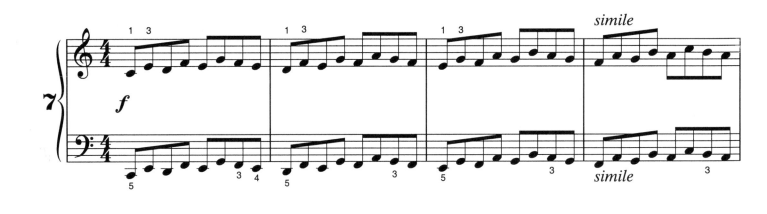

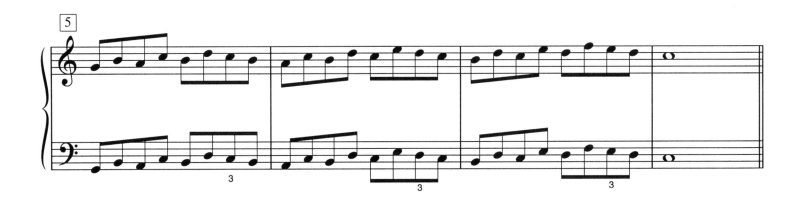

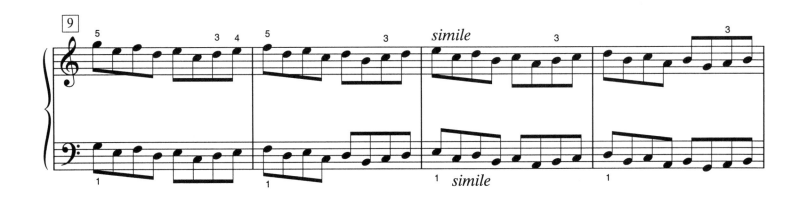

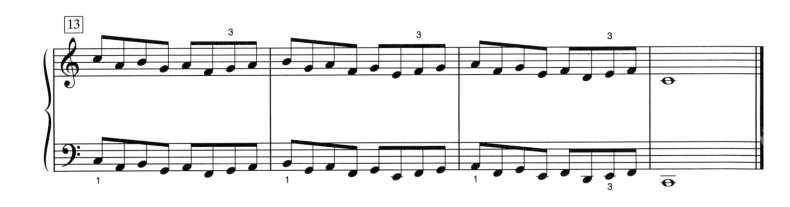

# No. 8

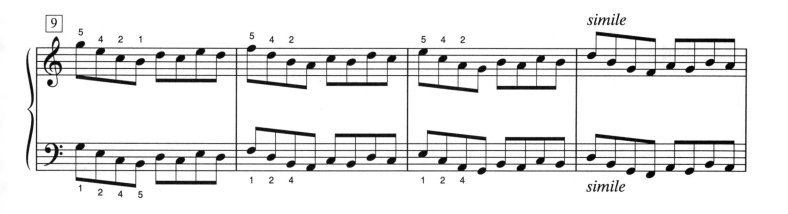

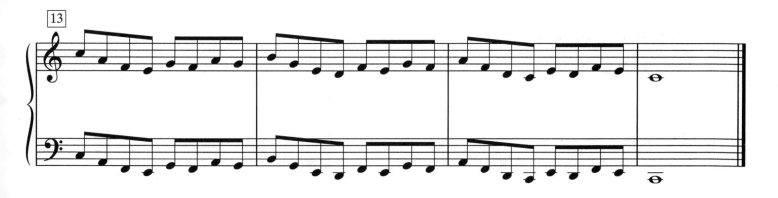

# No. 9

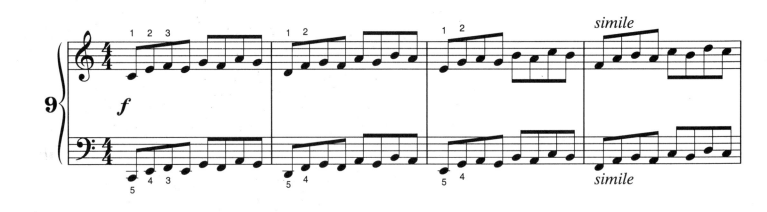

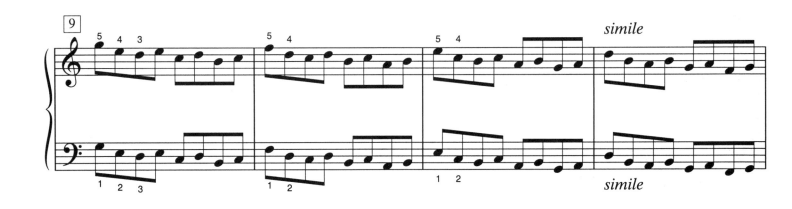

# No. 10

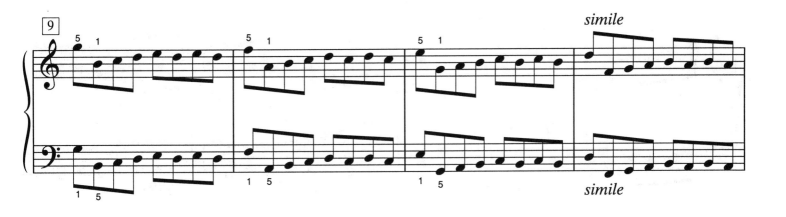

# No. 11

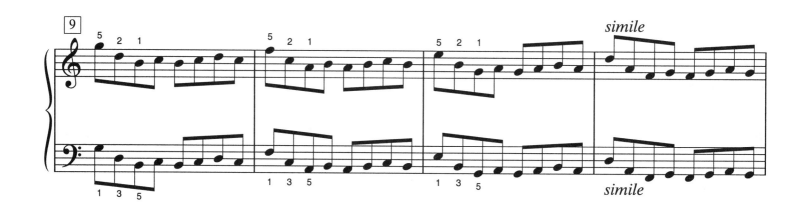

EL00208A

# No. 12

# No. 13

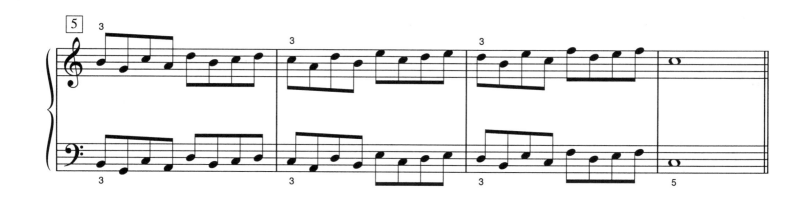

# No. 14

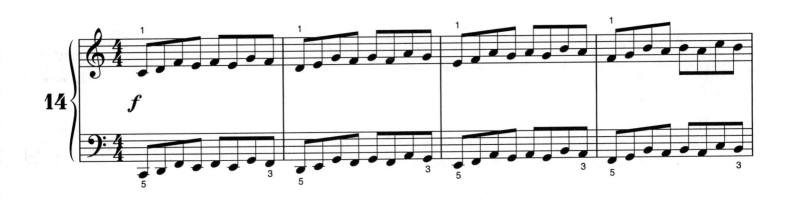

EL00208A

# No. 15

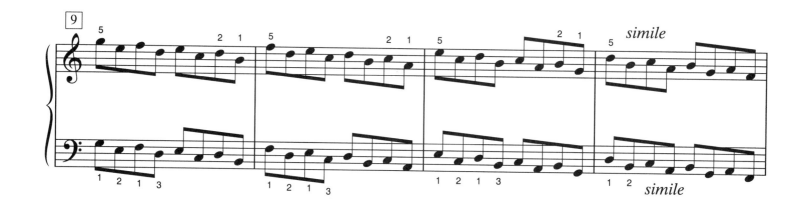

# No. 16

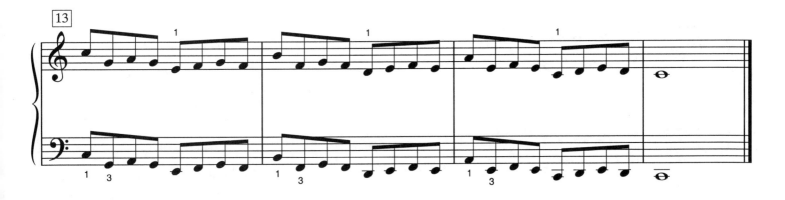

EL00208A

# No. 17

# No. 18

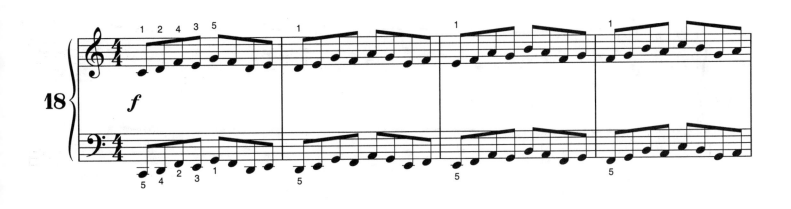

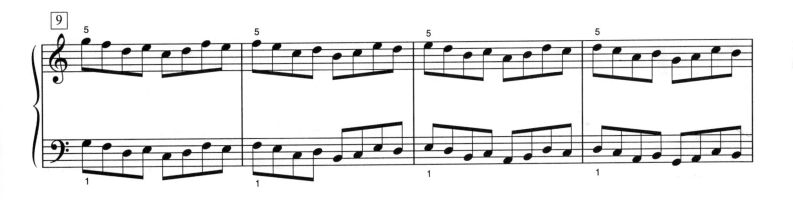

# No. 19

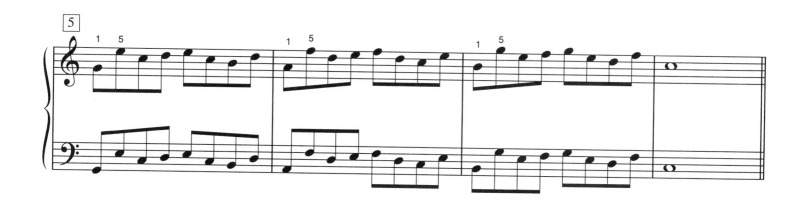

# No. 20

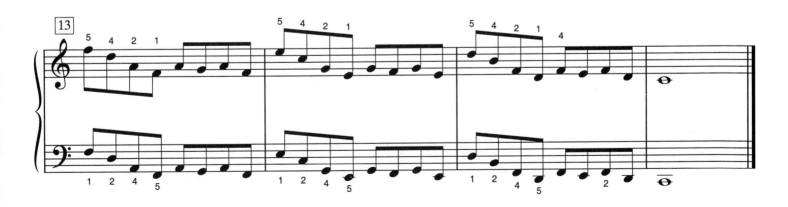

EL00208A

# No. 21

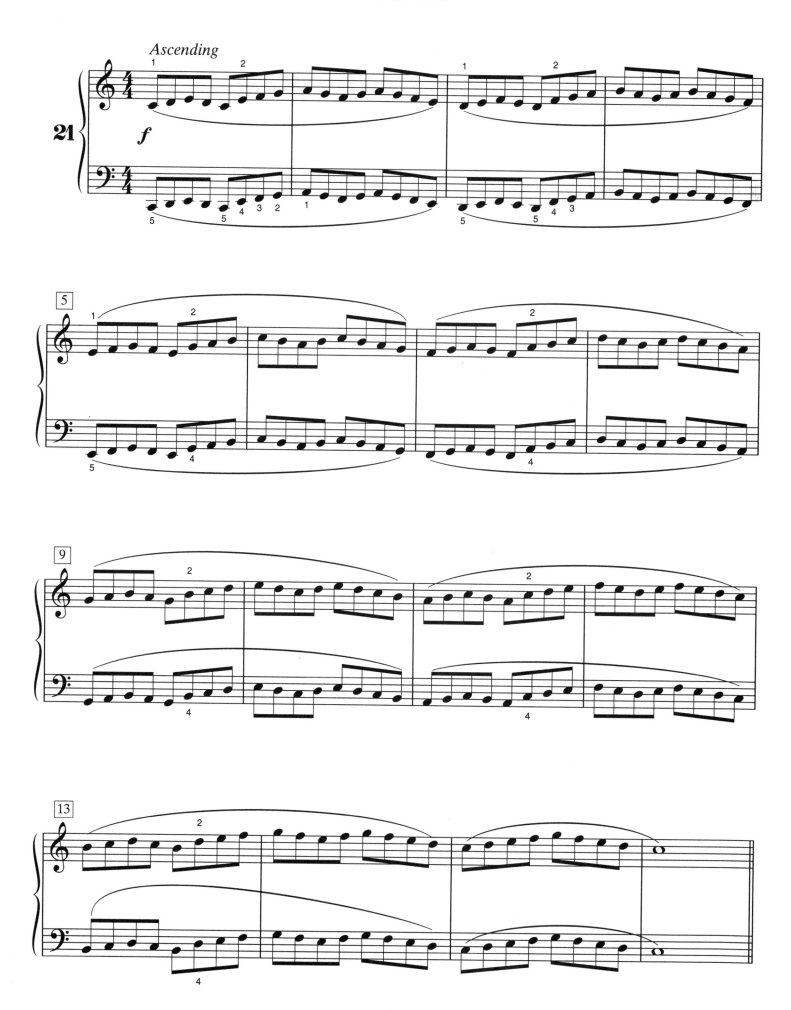

# No. 22

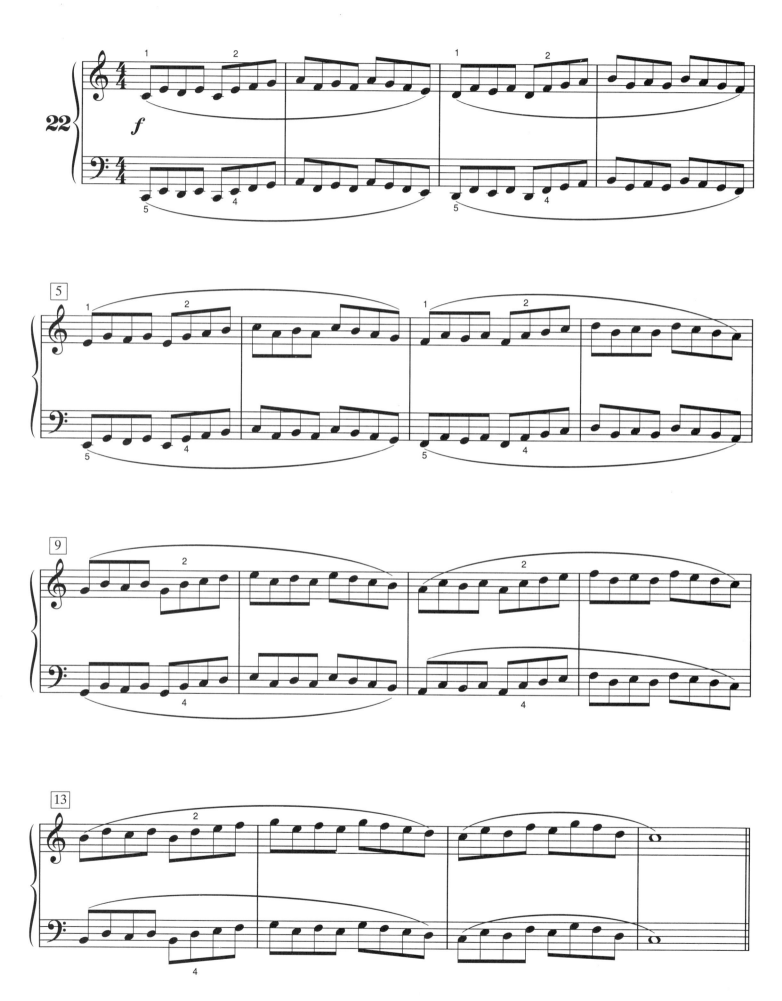

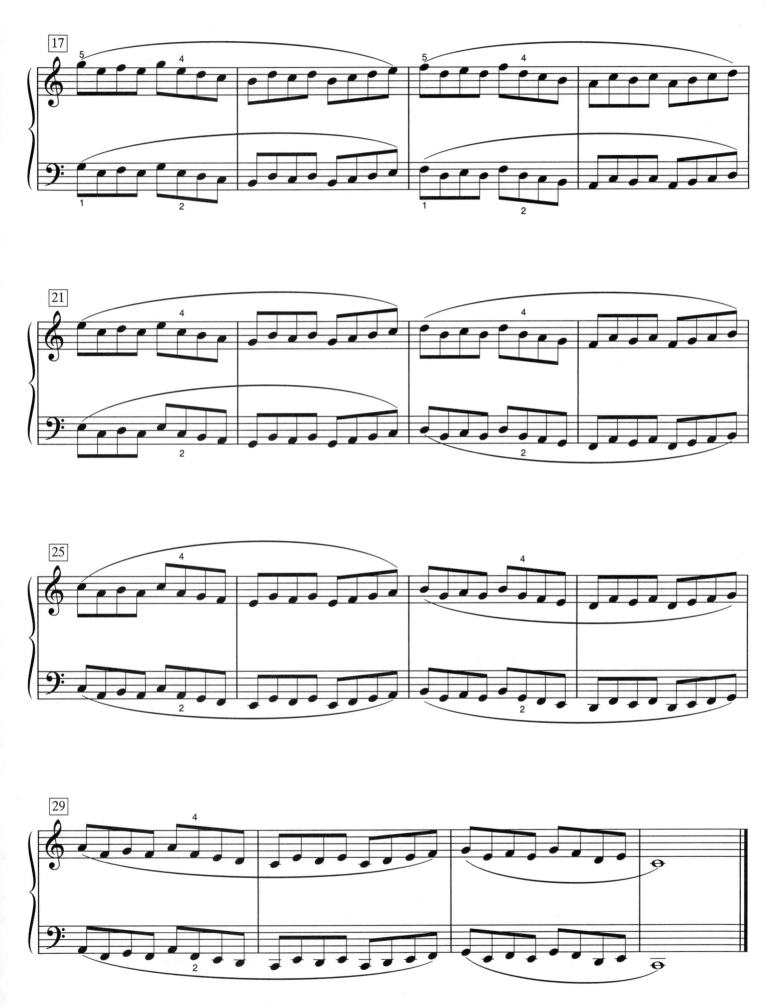

# No. 23

# No. 24

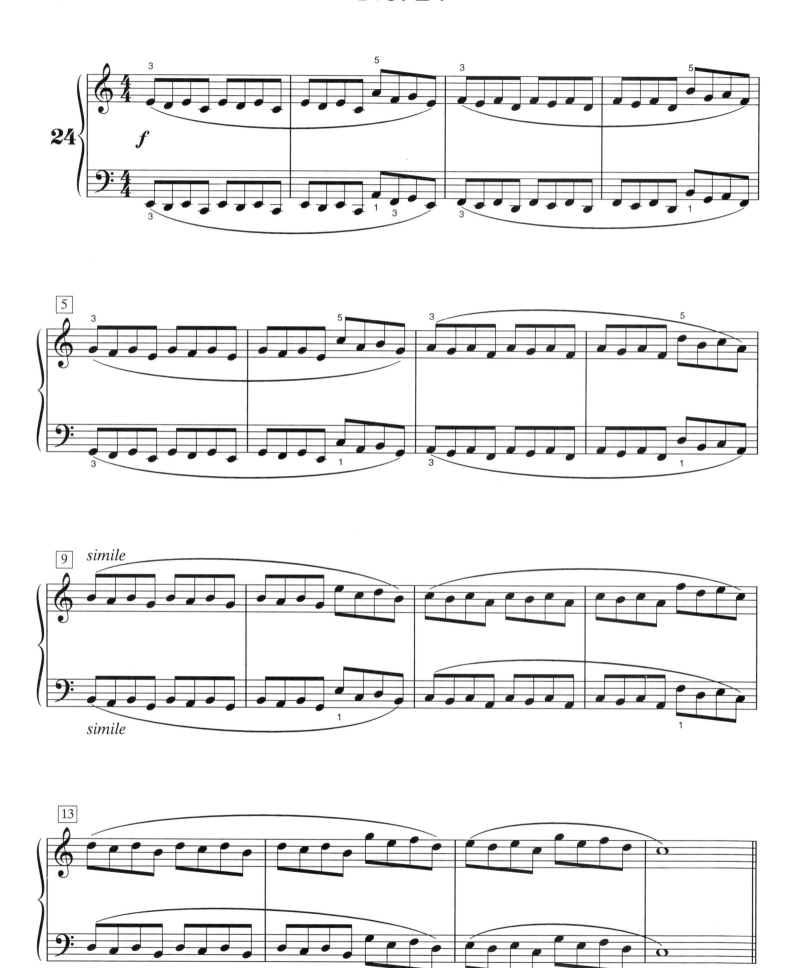

*You are now ready to begin Hanon-Schaum Book 2 (EL00209).

EL00208A

# John W. Schaum
# (1905–1988)

Founder and director of the Schaum Music School in Milwaukee, Wisconsin, John W. Schaum is the composer of internationally famous piano teaching materials including more than 200 books and 450 sheet music pieces. He is author of the internationally acclaimed *Schaum Piano Course* published by Belwin-Mills Publishing Corporation/Warner Bros. Publications. During his extensive travels, Mr. Schaum presented hundreds of piano teacher workshops in all fifty states. He was president of the Wisconsin Music Teachers Association and soloist with the Milwaukee Philharmonic Orchestra.

Mr. Schaum received a master of music degree from Northwestern University, a bachelor of music degree from Marquette University, and a bachelor of music education degree from the University of Wisconsin-Milwaukee.

He remains an important influence in the lives of hundreds of thousands of piano students who have enjoyed and continue to play his music.